NEVER

Give

UP

ROY and ANNE WHITT

ISBN 978-1-0980-5524-0 (paperback)
ISBN 978-1-0980-5525-7 (digital)

Christian Faith Publishing, Inc.
832 Park Avenue
Meadville, PA 16335
www.christianfaithpublishing.com

Printed in the United States of America

This story depicts the life of Roy Whitt and Anne Whitt, husband and wife. It is our intention to provide you with a glimpse into our individual as well as joint life, through the union of marriage. Here we recollect our lives before, during and after the transition of an unthinkable event, one that would shake and reshape us forever.

That which was sent to destroy us, caused us to become inextricably bound to not only each other, but more importantly bound to God. Even unto days when it all seems too real to be real in ways that are not understood.

This story is not an attempt to distort or pass judgment on those who were engaged in our lives before or after these events happened. But more importantly, it is our hope that this story provides an insight of our truth of understanding: for richer, for poorer, for better or for worse, in sickness and in health.

In the forthcoming pages, you will learn that without faith it is impossible to please God.

All scriptural references are taken from the King James Version and New King James Version, except where noted.

No harm is intended to anyone living or deceased. The story is designed to give God the glory that he deserves. We believe you will enjoy this story and perhaps even consider writing your story, for you, too, have been divinely created.

Write the Vision. Make it plain. (Habakkuk 2:2)

We dedicate this story of our lives as a testament to what God does. He sent the Comforter to us before we knew there would be a need. He has never left our side even when we were tossed to and fro and didn't know where to go or where we even were. We wish everyone the joy of getting to know Him.

To my Proverbs 31 wife, Anne, I would like to express my loving thanks, respect, and honor to you as you are my most valuable gift from God. I couldn't have chosen a better partner. You were there when many disappeared. You remained by my side even when I didn't know I was alive!

In sincere and thankful love,

Roy

Acknowledgments

We take this moment to acknowledge our children. There are times when we as adults, who endure the unexpected turns in our lives, simply don't realize the impact that those unexpected turns have on our children.

We would like to express to each one of our children how much we care and love them, for their patience and love through all of this.

To our children, many times we were impatient with you. It could not have been easy to see all that you saw and not be impacted by all that was going on around you. We are stronger now and could not have been so if it were not for you and your love:

Duane White
LaRenzo Harts
Sonya Baskerville
Nicole Coleman
Angela Whitt
Roy Whitt Jr.

And our deepest admiration to all those who have journeyed with us before and after these trials. Thank you.

Introduction

Marriage is a beautiful and sacred institution ordained by God for a man and his wife. When you think of marriage, you think of forever. We believe we will stand together daily, raising children, loving, and growing old together and beyond. We build. We plan. We believe we'll almost never experience any challenges. And if we do, we believe that they will be met and dealt with thanks to the strength of our bond.

So what happens when the unthinkable enters this perfect scenario?

It wasn't infidelity or death that took us by surprise but a savage and relentless entity that came out of nowhere—something that would rock us to the very core of our foundation.

Never in our wildest imaginations could we ever believe something such as this would occur in our lives.

Never!

This is the story of our lives, which has taken nearly forty years to come to fruition: the story of a love that endures.

Without faith it is impossible to please God.
—Hebrews 11:6

Looking Back to the Beginning

Train up a child in the way he should go, and
when he is old, he will not depart from it.
                                        —Proverbs 22:6

Our life as a family was one of diligence and dedication to keeping the family first in collective efforts, which was spearheaded by my father, Ruphus Whitt. Not only did my father believe in working hard, he also believed in hard work. He not only believed it for himself by being the head provider of our family, but he also made sure that he handled his responsibility for ensuring we had the necessities that we needed. My mother, of course was sure to take care of those responsibilities that were designated to her as a wife, in what most would refer to "women's work" of cooking and cleaning, being responsible for making sure the children were well, not wasting monies by always being frugal, and of course, making sure that she was attentive to her husband's needs. My father and mother were a unique team that reflected the love and respect they had for each other.

Growing up on a sharecropper's plantation wasn't a luxury at all. We had no running water, but thankfully we had an outside toilet. We worked so hard every single day. We were a close family and couldn't help but to be that way. In our two-bedroom house, us kids slept in a room with two beds in one room. There was another bed in the other room. Some of us slept at the head of the bed, and others slept at the foot of the bed. What we did was to get in where we fit in! We were close! My father and mother slept in the same room with the kids.

The walls in our house had cracks in them. We would tear up old magazines and make a paste from flour and water. Then we would paste the paper on the walls to keep the air out.

For fun on the weekends, my brother Joe and his friends would go *blind bird hunting*. They would bring the birds back, and we had fun putting them in the ashes in the fireplace and cook them.

Life on the sharecropper plantation wasn't much of a life, but we did have one another, and that was the best part of it all. We didn't get a fair share of our work, not at any time. You would have thought that by working so hard, we would at least get a fair and equitable split for our crops. That never happened. The crops that were grown by us was "shared" with the owner of the land. To obtain the fertilizer and various other supplies to plant crops, we had to purchase the fertilizer from the plantation owner in his store. At the end of the season, we had to pay him for everything that we had need of to plant the crops and harvest them as well. Everything that we needed had to be purchased on credit from the plantation owner. You can see that there was never a fifty-fifty deal; it was more like seventy-thirty or even eighty-twenty with us getting the short end of the stick every season.

My father was the type of man who was always concerned about his family's well-being. He took his responsibilities very seriously. My father was also a thinking man. Night after night, he would lay awake trying to think of ways that would put him and his family ahead of where we were, which was not too far along actually. How could it be, working and living under those conditions? It was in the late '40s and early '50s, and we lived in Alabama. What more can I say?

As the word *impossible* was not in my father's vocabulary, my father came up with a scheme to move off the plantation to his own land! He lay still, awake at night, thinking of the best ways that he would be able to execute on how to do what and when to do it too! My father wanted to escape with his family to a better life for us all.

Finally, his idea or his scheme, if you will, started out small and grew into a full-blown plan. My father decided to open a liquor still. He built it himself from scratch in the woods. He made a mash (a mixture of hot water and grains) to make the liquor. My father then dug large holes in the ground at home. He put fifty-gallon barrels in the ground and covered them up so that they were undetectable. We were able to walk over them, and at night, Father would take the mash in the woods to the still and run the liquor. Now to avoid people, he would wake up as early as 3:00 a.m. and deliver to his distributors.

As you may recall, I said my father believed in everyone working. That included me too, so from the young age of five years old, my father started to develop my work ethic. He certainly introduced me to hard work. My father ensured that my practical knowledge of working hard and hard work was in full effect. I can remember picking cotton at five years old. There was a big shade tree. My father made me a pallet and gave me a cotton sack made out of a fertilizer bag. I would pick cotton for a while and go back under the shade tree until I had picked thirty pounds of cotton. I even recall picking peanuts off the vine when the moon was out at night. Everyone—I mean everyone—had some work to do in my father's house. No one was exempt!

Daily Life

All day my father worked in the fields, and at night he ran the liquor still. My father utilized every moment of time to get things done. We were an enterprising family. We sold milk and okra on the street. At the age of six, I began school next to a church. The school was named after the church. We had to walk ten miles per day to school. Kids these days have it made! I don't think anyone walks that far to school anymore!

During this time, my father and mother saved up $7,000! Can you imagine? That was a huge sum of money for anyone during those times. Father and Mother were planning to build our own house and move off the plantation. My father's older brother had his own place in Beloit, Alabama. With the money that my parents saved, my father purchased two acres of land from my uncle, Arlue Whitt.

Both my father and brother cleared the land in preparation for building our home. After that, my father purchased a condemned home in the city of Selma, Alabama, and tore it down to use the lumber to build our new home in Beloit. My father was a resourceful man!

By that time, it was in 1951; and with some help, he secretly began construction on our new home. Our new home was finished within a year. Let me tell you, before the plantation owner could figure out anything, we were off their land and into our new home in Beloit, Alabama.

After moving off the plantation, my father continued to farm the plantation owner's land. However, I wasn't sure of the financial arrangement that was made. I'm assuming it was not a fifty-fifty deal as it was before. Our new home had a living room, a dining room, guest bedroom, and three other bedrooms.

Because my father did not get his education, he made sure that we did not miss one day of school. Actually, even when I was still six years old, he made sure that we did not miss school and that we had chores to do after school. Back in those days, if you got in trouble in school, your teachers sent you to the principal's office. The principal had a paddle with holes in it, and they would squeeze your pants leg tight while hitting your leg. If your parents found out that you were acting up in school and got disciplined, when you got home, you were getting disciplined again.

After we had moved into our new home, I was enrolled in Dallas County High School. We had to walk, but it wasn't far.

Hard Work Does Pay Off

Before long, my father purchased forty acres of woodland. He and my brother Joe cleared the timber off the land to sell. Once the land was cleared, he farmed six acres of his land. He then rented some of the land to other people to farm as well. At that time, your land had an allotment on it, which prevented you from farming all your land at one time. Father farmed cotton, corn, sweet potatoes, peanuts, okra, beans, and cucumbers. He also raised cows, pigs, and chickens.

You would think that our father would slack up a bit now that he had multiple streams of income coming in, but he didn't. Father wasn't idle at any time. If you looked in the dictionary for the definition of *hard work*, there must be a picture of my father. Father had lots of cows and fifteen acres of cotton. He rented land for hay to feed the cows and sold the rest. On Saturdays, we took truckloads of hay to a vendor's area to sell.

Before long, once again, my father started up his liquor still. Daddy built a smokehouse with all types of contraptions inside of it that would produce the liquor. He did this to support his family.

The women had it hard. The women had the responsibility of helping gather the crops and maintaining the house. Father still believed in my working hard, and as such, I had to plow the mule from sunup to sundown, five and a half days of the week during the crop season. You can imagine that on Saturdays, I was not a willing participant. My friends had the whole day to have fun; I had to work a half day on a Saturday. They weren't a complete bust, though, because Father did allow me to earn my own money by cutting firewood and selling it. Little did I realize this was the beginning of my desire to provide for myself and perhaps a family one day for my future. The money I made from selling firewood would sometimes be spent on buying suits for school. I loved wearing suits even at an early age. I didn't realize it then, but I guess you can say that my daddy took me everywhere with him when I was growing up for me to learn about life.

When I was eleven years old, my father and I went on a special trip. Father purchased a new 1957 Chevrolet truck. During my fifteenth year, my father allowed me to borrow the truck. A couple of my buddies and I were hauling hay. I began to show off, causing us to get into an accident. The truck rolled over roughly three times, but luckily, no one was hurt. When the accident happened, my father was in the swamp waiting for me to bring the hay. Someone informed him that I had been in an accident. Daddy made his way out of the swamp to the scene of the accident. The state police was called, and my father took the rap as if he had the accident because I was underage.

> *He who covers a transgression seeks love, but*
> *he who repeats a matter separates friends.*
> —Proverbs 17:9

The insurance would not have paid for damages if my father had not covered me with his love.

School Memories

In 1961 a new school was constructed in the woods approximately fifteen miles from the Dallas County High School. Construction of the new school began because a new law had been passed stating that whites could no longer pass one school to get to another. Since Dallas County High was on the main drag, the whites would have had to attend the all black school. As a result, Dallas County High was closed and Hazel Hall High was constructed. I attended Hazel Hall High from the ninth to the twelfth grade.

Once I turned sixteen, my father bought a tractor, which I used at night to till other people's land to earn money. Out of the money that was earned we paid for the gas and split the profit. During my spare times, I went to work for my cousin for four dollars per day for extra money. My father was proud of me; I certainly was not afraid of hard work just like he taught me.

Testing the Water, a Man Emerges

It was in July 1964 that I left for Connecticut. I was eighteen years old. My father took me to the Greyhound Bus Station and dropped me off. This was the beginning of a new journey and I was venturing out to see what adult life in the city had to offer me. Here I was, a young man setting out to discover a whole new world of possibilities. I had been in training in my father's home from the time I was five years old. My father demonstrated to us daily what it meant to be a provider and head of household. My mother encouraged my father, and I truly believed that is what inspired him. They depended on God first and then on one another. My father left no stones unturned. I had learned a lot watching my father and mother. I did my fair share of working and contributing too. I had reaped bountifully in ways that cannot be counted or perhaps understood even.

> *For now we see in a mirror, dimly, but then*
> *face to face. Now I know in part, but then*
> *I shall know just as I also am known.*
> —1 Corinthians 13:12

It took me three days to travel from Selma, Alabama, to Hartford, Connecticut. My older brother Joe picked me up from the bus station. I moved in with him and his family on Hampton Street, which was in a housing project named Stowe Village.

Joe was doing well working at Waybest Packing Company where he was a supervisor. My brother was my boss for nine months. After working there for only three months at Waybest, I had saved enough money to purchase my first car. Oh man, was I proud of my 1960 Chevy Convertible! Unfortunately, during that time, an eighteen-year-old could not register a car in their own name. The legal age to register a vehicle was twenty-one.

In light of this legality, Joe registered the vehicle in his name. I was so proud of my shiny white Chevy Convertible. I financed the Chevy for two years through General Motors. By financing the vehicle, I was able to establish my credit. In 1967, after I paid the Chevy off, I had established enough credit to purchase a 1966 Pontiac GTO in my own name.

Working steadily at Waybest, my hourly wages were $1.25 per hour. After nine months of working there, I began to seek a better-paying job. The situation was really getting to me, but I didn't want to impose on my brother and his family again. I would wash myself at the Institute of Living. Before you knew it, I started working at the Institute of Living on Washington Street in Hartford. I worked in the housekeeping department. I was responsible for delivering items to the residents of this senior housing development. My beginning hourly wage was $1.50. Although I was earning $10.00 per week, I was still not satisfied with my pay. Not being one to settle, I started working a second job at Lock Joint Pipe Company in Newington. The pay there was $2 an hour. I worked from 7:00 a.m. to 11:00 a.m. Monday through Friday. I worked two jobs for approximately two years.

Is There a Better Way?

While I worked both jobs, I began saving money from my second job. I was getting tired of working those long hours. I began thinking about what I needed to do. I decided to stop working for approximately one month.

I lived with my brother Joe and his family for three months when I decided that it was time to move. My coworker Bobby from Waybest and I decided to get an apartment together. We rented a two-bedroom apartment on Wooster Street. This was not the best idea. After staying there for a while, Bobby moved in with his girlfriend, and I could not handle paying the rent on my own.

Then there came an opportunity with two of my associates to sublet an apartment from a guy name CeCe Whitehead on Magnolia Street in Hartford. We were paying the rent directly to CeCe. Of course, CeCe was pocketing the money, and we were evicted from this apartment.

I was homeless for one month and had to sleep in my car. This situation was getting to me, but I didn't want to infringe on my brother and his family. I would wash myself at the Institute of Living.

Enter the Sisters

My sister Delores introduced me to a friend of hers by the name of Alma Collins. Alma had two brothers: Leo and John. Leo, John, and I rented an apartment on Bedford Street in Hartford. While living on Bedford Street, I met this girl by the name of Martha. Prior to dating me, Martha used to go out with this guy named Gene Rivers, who owned a restaurant on Albany Avenue. Gene seemed like he had more influence over Martha than I did, and I became jealous. I am not certain if my jealousy stemmed from him being in business for himself or if it was about his influence over Martha.

Jealousy or no jealousy, I began to prepare myself financially to be in business for myself. Not long into the relationship, Martha and I broke up. Later, I would meet Hazel. Hazel and I dated for a while, and then we moved in together. Shortly after, Hazel gave birth to my oldest daughter, Sonya Baskerville. Soon after, I got a new job at Chandler Evans Company on New Park Avenue in West Hartford. Chandler Evans manufactured carburetors and pumps for aircrafts. They also reconditioned old carburetors and pumps. It was a good-paying job at $2.50 per hour. While working at Chandler Evans, I was able to save $10,000 and opened my first restaurant. What an accomplishment! I continued working nights at Chandler Evans; after all, I am my father's son.

Hazel and my sister Unzia were running the restaurant while I worked at night. This continued until the day Martin Luther King Jr. was assassinated on April 4, 1968. There was so much rioting going on at the time, and Hazel and Unzia were afraid to be at the restaurant alone. I had to quit my job at Chandler Evans and began to work at the restaurant full-time. The restaurant was called Roy's Restaurant and Dairy and was located on Albany Avenue. The business didn't do well. We operated the business for one year. After weighing my options, I decided to go to the black-owned bank which was headed by Ed Barlow. I attempted to obtain a business loan; however, the bank was only a mortgage loan bank, and they did not specialize in commercial loans. Ed Barlow referred me to Hartford National Bank on Woodland Street, where they had a minority business loan program, and that bank loaned me $2,000.

Even after obtaining the loan, I could not generate enough business and was forced to sell the business. I sold the business to a Muslim gentleman who assumed the balance of the two-thousand-dollar loan. After the sale of the restaurant, I was propositioned by the owner of Pat's Bakery located on the corner of Garden and Mather Streets. The owners let me take over the restaurant located in the front of their bakery. I sold chili hot dogs, chili hamburgers, and fish sandwiches. I ran the business up until the building caught fire. Unfortunately, I did not have any insurance, so I lost everything.

To alleviate some of my bills, I traded my Pontiac GTO for a Rambler. The guy I traded with assumed the remaining payments on the GTO. The Rambler broke down, so I bought a 1966 Buick. I had saved approximately $2,000 while I was in business. After the burger business burned, I started looking for a new building. I found a building on the corner of Nelson and Clay Street, which had been vacant for years. I found out that the owner of the building was C. H. Blanks. I began renting the store front. There were many repairs that needed to be done; and of course, I began making the repairs. At that time, the monthly rent was $50. There was some equipment already in place, and I refurbished that equipment. There was still a need for more equipment. A Jewish guy by the name of Phil Klein financed some equipment, which I paid for on a weekly basis. Phil sold paper supplies for the store as well.

All in all, it took approximately a month to get the needed repairs done in preparation of the grand opening. The repairs had depleted a good portion of my cash. Because of this, I would purchase my stock daily. I would go to the wholesale stores and buy one-half cases of whatever I needed until I built my cash flow back up. I did this for about one year, and during this time, the business did well and thrived.

Collin Bennett, who was a local real estate agent, approached me about purchasing a home. At that time, my business paperwork was not in order. Collin put me in touch with his accountant to prepare my business statements so that I had my annual revenue on paper to approach the bank about a mortgage loan. I was then able to purchase my first home. This was a three-family at 205 Cornwall Street in Hartford. Approximately a month after I purchased my house, I bought a light-brown 1970 Lincoln Continental.

Things were going along so well that I caught the attention of the FBI, and they came to check the VIN under the hood of my Lincoln to see if it was a stolen vehicle. Apparently, someone had called them. I guess people were wondering how my small 35×35 square foot store was generating so much revenue.

> *And you shall remember the LORD your God,*
> *for it is He who gives you power to get wealth,*
> *that He may establish His covenant which*
> *He swore to your fathers, as it is this day.*
> —Deuteronomy 8:18

This store was located across from Nelton Court Housing Project. My store continued to do well. Because of this, I was being investigated. Undercover officers approached me and attempted to sell me drugs. Apparently, it was thought that my success was not based solely on the revenue of the store. It was assumed that I had to be dealing drugs. Being a country boy, I had never been introduced to the drug scene. I must admit, however, that the deal seemed tempting by the profits that were proposed to me. I refused the deal because I did not trust this stranger with my money. Thank you, Lord, that I did not fall into the trap.

> *For He shall give His angels charge over*
> *you, to keep you in all your ways.*
> —Psalm 91:11

Later I would learn that had I entered into this deal, I could have been arrested for drug trafficking. Even after the refusal of the drug deal, I was still being investigated. The police came to the store and asked about them searching the basement. Because I had nothing to hide, I complied.

> *Submit to Government—Let every soul be*
> *subject to the governing authorities. For*
> *there is no authority except from God, and*
> *the authorities that exist are appointed by*
> *God. Therefore whoever resists the authority*
> *resists the ordinance of God, and those who*
> *resist will bring judgment on themselves.*
> —Romans 13:1–2

And Suddenly She Appeared

In 1971, I went to the After Dark Night Club located at 463 Albany Avenue. A woman by the name of Lee Martin introduced me to a woman named Anne Harts. We began dating for about six months when she started renting an apartment on Westland Street. Two months after Anne got the apartment, we moved in together. Anne had a five-year-old son named LaRenzo. We stayed there in the apartment for a while, and after things became serious, I asked Anne to move into my home on Cornwall Street. Anne and LaRenzo moved in soon after.

> *"The voice of joy and the voice of gladness, the*
> *voice of the bridegroom and the voice of the*
> *bride, the voice of those who will say: 'Praise*
> *the LORD of hosts, For the LORD is good,*
> *For His mercy endures forever'—and of those who*
> *will bring the sacrifice of praise into the house*
> *of the LORD. For I will cause the captives of the*
> *land to return as at the first," says the LORD.*
> *—Jeremiah 33:11*

We all lived together for about one year before getting married in 1972. Anne wanted to drive my Lincoln, but she didn't have a license. I refused to let her drive until she got her license. She already knew how to drive but was not legally allowed to do so. She quickly got her license and started driving the Lincoln!

About a year later, in 1973, Anne gave birth to my second daughter, Nicole Whitt. By that time, it was time to get Anne a car. I purchased her a '69 VW Beetle. I needed to make sure that both she and the baby had transportation. We were still living on Cornwall Street, and I purchased a 1969 Sports Convertible. Later that year, I traded in both my 1970 Lincoln Continental and 1969 Jaguar for a 1973 Lincoln Continental.

A year later, my third daughter, Angela, was born in 1974. As our family grew, it was evident that it was time for us to have a single-family home. We purchased our first single-family at 152 Willowcrest Drive in Windsor, Connecticut, on May of 1975. I was happy, Anne was happy, the children were happy, and we were very proud of our beautiful raised ranch. I was providing for my family just as my father did for his family. Once we were settled in our new home, I began moving forward with the expansion of the business.

Next stop: we opened a Laundromat on Main Street, which burned down shortly after I opened the doors. The Laundromat had only been opened a little over a year when one of the dryers sparked fire and subsequently caused the entire business to burn down.

Advancing Our Position

Before you knew what had hit, I opened another grocery store on Main Street. I received financial backing from Gare Brothers Wholesalers in Windsor, Connecticut. The line of credit was so extensive that I did not have to obtain a loan from the bank.

Once again, Phil Klein furnished the equipment that I needed to operate the store. Roy's Grocery II was opened in 1976. I was able to pay for the equipment on a weekly basis.

Our household grew even more when my brother-in-law Darrell Harts moved in with us on Willowcrest Drive. Before long, I purchased Anne a 1976 Ford Granada. Anne had the car for approximately six months when Darrell was driving the car and got into an automobile accident, which resulted in a total loss. After the Granada was totaled, Anne drove an older station wagon. People were gossiping about the fact that Anne was driving an older vehicle, so I surprised her with a 1977 Ford Thunderbird.

The Lord blessed us once again with a beautiful child. Anne gave birth to my namesake, Roy Leon Whitt Jr., in 1977.

Our grocery store Roy's Grocery II was not doing well at all, so I decided to close the Main Street store. Still having the vision to expand our business, I then took over a record store which was previously owned by my cousin, Nate Robinson. The name of the record store was Nate's Record Shop. That business did not succeed either, so I closed the doors in 1978, but I wasn't giving up! As it would happen, I came across another opportunity as I laid my eyes on a storefront that was up for sale on Albany Avenue in Hartford, Connecticut.

The store was on the market for $25,000 for quite some time but did not sell. It was located on the corner of Magnolia Street and Albany Avenue. The owner of the building was anxious to sell, and he dropped the price to $20,000. After thinking about it, I decided to take the plunge, and I purchased the store.

Within two days of purchasing the store, I was able to get the store cleaned, stocked, and ready for business. The store had taken off great: the revenue was in excess of $13,000 a week. We were doing extremely well.

But there's always something that comes up to put you on edge. During this time, nearly three months after we opened the storefront, the white landlord, fearing for his safety, wanted to sell the building also because of rioting. The landlord pressured me into taking ownership of the entire building, which consisted of five additional storefronts and twelve apartments. There was no other recourse at the time than to assume a $56,000 loan directly from the bank and a $44,000 loan from the previous owner of the building.

Even with these matters going on, which involved a great deal of financial debt, the businesses were doing exceedingly well, and they were growing quickly. Approximately six months after the purchase of the Albany Avenue building, I purchased an apartment building on Magnolia Street in Hartford.

Our family was fully enlarged, and I wanted Anne and the children to be comfortable in a more spacious home. Anne and I discussed these matters and came to the decision that our next move was to purchase a larger home. We purchased a nine-room home in West Hartford. It was a truly beautiful lakefront property. When we initially tried to purchase the property, we encountered numerous issues. We did not anticipate the depth of opposition that we would face from some of our neighboring white homeowners.

God watched over us as always through every situation we encountered. My credit was excellent with no delinquencies, but it still took us well over two months to get the loan. I threatened the bank with a lawsuit, and the day after, the loan was approved. We were the first black family in the neighborhood. A few of the neighbors sold their homes after we moved into the neighborhood. One morning, I woke up to eggs smashed on my car. Someone even phoned the police to report that I had a commercial vehicle parked in my driveway. As a result, I had to reregister my vehicle as a personal-use vehicle.

On any given moment, there were challenges from the neighbors who lived next door. The neighbor asked my wife, Anne, to put our dog inside when they had guests. I thought to myself, who the heck did they think they were?

Being in the privacy of my own home, which was obtained through hard work and sacrifice, I was confronted by an officer. I was in my backyard fishing when this officer confronted me about what I was doing. When I explained that I was the owner, I no longer had problems with the local police force. I supposed that the neighbors could not conceive how a black man could own property in that neighborhood.

To further establish and advance our holdings, I made several purchases. The building that we rented on Nelson Street, we purchased. That property had four apartments. Right on the heels of that purchase, I purchased another grocery business on Capen Street for $20,000. For this purchase, I paid cash up-front. And again, Gare Brothers provided me with a line of credit which allowed me to stock the store. I would pay a percentage of what was credited and pay weekly for my current inventory.

We had three grocery stores! I decided to incorporate them. My hard work and working hard was paying off. My father is proud of me! I named the corporation Roy Whitt Enterprises. What in the world did I do that for? I was a target and on everyone's radar, including the bigwigs downtown. They were hot, mad, and after me! I didn't have a clue as to why at first. I can only fathom that this was because I am a black man, and I was not into the entertainment business or sports. I was certainly not dealing drugs that there must be some illegitimate matters going on with me to be this successful.

It must be that I have connections to the Mob because I grew like rapid fire without any bank backing. The only loan that I had ever had with a bank was for the $2,000 I took years ago. Life lessons were learned particularly when I opened the restaurant business. I found out how the system was for black people and especially for blacks who were in business. The playing field was not even at all. I bet not a one of them ever thought to consider the true facts about just being blessed and favored by God.

We Are Family

Many of my family members worked in the stores. There were five of my brother's children who worked in the stores. The teenagers did not want to be labored with working in any of the businesses. Thankfully, their parents, my brother and sister-in-law, insisted that they help in the stores. They were young and had the same challenges I did, so I could relate. I remember how upset I was by having to work on those half day Saturdays. They were very similar in their dissatisfaction with having to work at the stores even on the weekend.

My brother's children, Yvonne, Shirley, Pam, Rhonda, and Wayne along with my sister-in-law's son, Gary, did not appreciate the experience until they were adults. My brother saved a percentage of his children's earnings and gave it to them once they came of age. That is when their perspective changed. It definitely taught them good work ethics.

As a black man, it didn't matter what my net worth was in the business world that the white men dominated. To them, I was still less than they were, and I could never achieve the pinnacles of success that they had in their eyes. Thank God, I did, though. In actuality, I had more than most of them. This is not bragging nor boasting; it's the sheer fact that the Lord had enlarged my efforts and endeavors to nearly mammoth proportions. This is the Lord's doing. I was simply trying to be a good steward over what He's entrusted to me.

My father was subjected to these idiotic rules and regulations also. Back then, doing business with whites was no laughing matter—and one had to do business with the white man in order to survive.

In hindsight, my father endured more than his share of unfair circumstances because of the times and places where he resided. My father was a part of the plantation mentality at times. But not always, because he did break free to some degree to provide for his family. My parents did well. But my father worked too much. I know, I know, you're thinking, "Well, you're a chip off the old block," and I am. But I would like to believe and do believe that because of my being in the North, there was a distinct advantage of how I progressed. Take, for instance, my father being in the South and having to work under the cover of darkness in the middle of the night and having to work under all extremes of weather conditions just to get ahead for perhaps something as little as a dollar. It wasn't fair. However, my father endured all of it. He taught me to stand up even in hard times.

In Connecticut, I had more opportunities presented to me, and I advanced the line for my family at every turn that I could. I did not cheat, steal, or lie to get ahead. I simply developed my motto from being near my father, and that was to—*never give up!*

Go In and Possess the Land

After the death of Moses the servant of the LORD,
it came to pass that the LORD spoke to Joshua
the son of Nun, Moses' assistant, saying: "Moses
My servant is dead. Now therefore, arise, go over
this Jordan, you and all this people, to the land
which I am giving to them—the children of
Israel. Every place that the sole of your foot will
tread upon I have given you, as I said to Moses.
From the wilderness and this Lebanon as far as
the great river, the River Euphrates, all the land
of the Hittites, and to the Great Sea toward the
going down of the sun, shall be your territory. No
man shall be able to stand before you all the days
of your life; as I was with Moses, so I will be with
you. I will not leave you nor forsake you. Be strong
and of good courage, for to this people you shall
divide as an inheritance the land which I swore to
their fathers to give them. Only be strong and very
courageous, that you may observe to do according

to all the law which Moses My servant commanded
you; do not turn from it to the right hand or to
the left, that you may prosper wherever you go.
This Book of the Law shall not depart from your
mouth, but you shall meditate in it day and night,
that you may observe to do according to all that
is written in it. For then you will make your way
prosperous, and then you will have good success.
Have I not commanded you? Be strong and of good
courage; do not be afraid, nor be dismayed, for
the LORD *your God is with you wherever you go."*

—Joshua 1

After purchasing the building on Nelson and Capen Street I made yet another purchase, a twelve family house on Lenox Street. My property had many Latino tenants. I began to remodel the apartments, which required one of the Latino tenants to relocate. The city seemingly tried to set me up to and to make it seem like I was prejudiced toward the Latino community. Nothing could have been further from the truth. What the city wanted to do was distract me while disrupting my business by deterring my Latino customers from purchasing anything from my store.

On one occasion, they had the unmitigated gall to send a camera crew from the news media to my apartment building to take pictures of the remodeled apartment. They were trying to verify if I was indeed remodeling the apartment or getting rid of the Latino tenant through covert and prejudiced methods. There was nothing being done that would justify there was any wrongdoings. The camera crew had to turn around and depart from the premises the same way the entered—with nothing. The investigation was halted; there was nothing found out of order. I was in total compliance.

Things continued to move along. I hadn't made any residential or commercial acquisitions of late. My grocery store needed some repairs. My cash flow was somewhat sluggish for the moment. The empty apartments above the store were vandalized. Fortunately, the insurance company paid for the repair costs. The bank, in turn, took the money from the insurance company and gave me clear title of the building. In the meantime, I needed about $40,000 to renovate the entire building.

I went to a gambling casino called the HiLi after closing the store and won $50,000. I used that $50,000 to make those repairs and renovations on the property.

My family and I worked diligently. I've worked hard in every manner to take care of my family. There could be no other dream position that would be suited for me. This is my life; this is the way God planned it.

At times, it's hard to believe as I look back on all that the Lord has allowed me to do. My lif has been truly blessed in more ways than one.

Becoming More Than Expected

Shortly thereafter, I bought a six-family house on Homestead Avenue for $3,500 and the property was $3,000 in back taxes. I spent approximately $45,000 to remodel and renovate the property. It seemed like it would be a lucrative opportunity for me to further advance my real estate holdings.

I owned three stores but had grown tired of running from store to store, having to close them. By now you can imagine my thought processes. Yes, you guessed it! Tiredness was setting in. I was literally wearing myself out running all over town. I was doing my best to keep everything running smooth. As God would have it, I was able to find another store on Washington Street in Hartford, Connecticut, but to my disappointment, they would not lease it to me either. However, they did lease it to a Spanish man. The name of the store was Artez's Grocery.

The city proposed building a mall further up on Albany Avenue; the mall consortium was seeking tenants. It wasn't long before I began my search for one big store. Wouldn't you know, it wasn't long until I ended up finding a store on Main Street which had closed, but the owners would not sell it to me.

There was a very large building for sale on Albany Avenue, which happened to be the location of the first black bank in Hartford. This bank had relocated to downtown Hartford. In order to purchase the building, I had to lie about my intentions on the use of the building so the owners wouldn't turn me down. When asked what I was doing with the building, I told them that I was using it as a warehouse to supply my other stores. They agreed to sell me the building for $350,000. (Note: money isn't everything, God is all of everything. He owns the cattle on a thousand hill, and you're His child. Have faith. God is the Provider. If I could do it in those days, today you certainly can do it too. I know what I'm talking about, and I encourage you to get things in order and just begin to do. He'll guide you through.)

My lawyer found out that the insurance company owned the building, so I had to put $25,000 down. I was the contractor, having learned everything from Ben Brown over the years by watching him. After the removal of the bricks, I called the housing inspector. He told me that I needed an architect to draw up blueprints for the building. I hired an architect from Bloomfield to do the blueprints. The work came to a halt for three months until the architect finished his work. My friend Ben Brown got a permit on the building to start the renovations. Three layers of brick wall had to be removed from the center of the building. I hired some street workers to help me gut the inside of the building. After completion of the blueprints, I proceeded with the renovations. When the layers of brick were removed, I spent another $3,000 for an ironworker to place a steel beam for support. I spent roughly $300,000 of my own money to pay for renovations. I had to borrow $200,000 from SBA Loans to place equipment in the store.

Due to politics, the banks refused to participate through the SBA. I had to go through a money store to get the money from SBA. The payment on the loan from SBA was $1,600 a month. The same wholesaler, Sweetlife Wholesale, located in Wilson, Connecticut, that was supplying Blanchard's Food refused to supply me. Blanchard's already had a store on Barber Street in Hartford. I had to go out of town to get a wholesaler to supply my store. The name of the wholesaler was Buzzuto Wholesaler, located in Stanford, Connecticut. Initially, they stocked my store for $200,000.

Let's remember the times that we were in. It wasn't as favorable as it could have been or should have been to be a black man in a lucrative business with a strong financial bottom line. This was, of course, due to the politics of the time and era and all that red tape involved. Apparently, I didn't have the right connections. Even though they tried to deter me for some reason, at every turn that was wrought with letdown after letdown, no matter what, I was still determined to get my *big* store. Let me stop here for a moment and say something to you. If you have a dream, it doesn't matter how small it is or seems, continue to pursue that dream. It's who you are. It is the road that you're to travel to get where the Lord is leading you. I can tell you, when I look back now with a very different perspective, only God could have known what the end was going to be like. And still, after these things, He still causes me to desire to continue to pursue my dreams.

There were many obstacles which seemed to hinder me from getting to my next location, but I was determined to never give up. Once again, I was able to overcome.

Once the store was stocked, I set a date for the grand opening. The mayor at the time, Mayor Milner, Senator Wilbur Smith, the city manager, secretary of treasury, Reverend Wilson, and other dignitaries were present. WDRC radio station was the host for the grand opening. During the festivities, I ran a promotion where you purchased $50 worth of groceries and got a free turkey. Things were going great, and I was bringing in around $5,000 a day. We named the store Whitt's Discount Supermarket, located at 620 Albany Avenue. We were in business for about three months, taking business from all the surrounding big stores and suburbs. Prior to opening the supermarket, people in the surrounding communities had to go to the suburbs to shop because all the area supermarkets had left and moved to the suburbs. This left the people without a place to shop locally, which was why they were thrilled when Whitt's Discount Supermarket opened.

A Place To Shop, a Sign of Renewal

By DONARD SHERMAN
Courant Staff Writer

Residents of Hartford's Upper Albany neighborhood have been without a major supermarket for nearly a decade. But Wednesday, shoppers guided carts loaded with vegetables, sacks of potatoes, fruit and meats across the glistening floor of Roy L. Whitt's discount food center.

The 15,000-square-foot, red-brick supermarket at 620 Albany Ave. represents the latest advance in an effort to revitalize Albany Avenue, the North End's largest commercial strip.

"What I'm seeing here today is the beginning of a renaissance," said Hartford Mayor Thirman L. Milner, one of several city, state and community leaders who celebrated the grand opening of Whitt's Discount Foods.

Bicyclists pulled over and pedestrians gathered outdoors to hear the dignitaries speak through a public address system that competed with the roar of passing traffic.

"From the time we opened Roy's grocery store (on Nelson Street) in 1968, I believed we could do it," Whitt told the crowd. "I needed here. It's an uplift to the community," he said after the speech.

The city has seen more than 15 supermarkets close in the last 15 years, forcing residents to shop at supermarkets far from their homes, sometimes

Roy C. Whitt, wearing a boutonniere and a proud smile, shows off his new Albany Avenue market.

as far away as the suburbs. The last major food outlet in the Upper Albany area, Abe Giles's Supermarket, closed in February 1973.

Upper Albany has been in a state of flux for decades. In the 1960s and 1970s, most of the then-predominantly white population left for the suburbs as poorer blacks and Hispanics moved in. Riots in the late 1960s and early 1970s and deteriorated housing conditions devastated sections of the neighborhood.

But the area recently has been undergoing a more encouraging metamorphosis.

Housing has been rehabilitated on many side streets, several store owners have spruced up their shops and a $125,000 bakery opened at 1297 Albany Ave. in 1981.

Officials from the Upper Albany Community Organization also are trying to develop a new multi-million-dollar supermarket and shopping center near the intersection of Albany Ave-

See A Place, Page C2

was charged with one count of gambling and two counts of using the telephone to transmit or receive gambling information. Those charges are misdemeanors and carry, respectively, maximum terms of six months and a year in jail.

His arrest came five days after Torrington Police Chief Dominic Antonelli, 54, was arrested by state police. The chief was charged Saturday with professional gambling and conspiracy.

While the two arrests are part of the same three-month investigation, "there is no direct tie-in between the chief (Antonelli) and Soliani," said State Police Sgt. Bruce Russo, commanding officer of the Statewide Organized Crime Investigative Task Force.

Conversations involving the two police officers were picked up on two of four separate wiretaps resulting in police raids at seven city homes within four days, said Russo.

The wiretaps, said police, disclosed that none of the bets were placed from either the police station or from the Canaan state police barracks where Soliani works. Authorities also said that no other police officers are suspects in the investigation.

Soliani was suspended without pay immediately after he surrendered to detectives at task force headquarters. Soliani was released without a cash bond for his appearance in Torrington Superior Court Sept. 27.

Antonelli's arrest has not yet resulted in an investigation of the city force because Mayor Michael Conway said such action would be premature while the state police probe continues. Charged with 15 gambling counts, he is scheduled to appear Sept. 27 in Litchfield Superior Court.

After Antonelli was released without bond Saturday, Conway relieved him of his command, pending a special hearing before the Board of Public Safety Saturday at 9 a.m.

That hearing, which can be a secret session at the chief's request, is necessary under the city charter before Antonelli can be demoted, suspended or fired.

Once my store opened, there were rumors circulating that the city was thinking about cancelling the upper Albany Avenue supermarket project. The powers that be began feeling threatened that the multimillion-dollar project on Albany Avenue was going to be cancelled. I believe this led them to set my store on fire. After leaving my store around eight thirty that night, I received a phone call a few hours later from the security monitoring center that my building was on fire. Afterward, I rushed down to the store, horrified to find my building in flames.

Fortunately, I had not closed Whitt's Supermarket and it was still operating on Capen Street in Hartford. The wholesaler would not give me credit to fill the store with groceries, so I had to pay cash. Luckily, I still had the license for the A&M Market and Roy's Groceries because the city was giving me a hard time regenerating my businesses. The landlord decided to sell the building located under my store on Capen Street, thereby forcing me to move out quicker than I needed to or was ready for. During that time, I was remodeling A&M Market.

Keep your head on straight and try to have a backup plan. Strategy is essential. Since they deemed that I was to move so quickly, I moved all my merchandise from Capen Street to the A&M Market. The electric company would not turn the lights on in my A&M Market because I owed them money. Instead, I used my store manager's name with his consent to get the lights turned on. Once again, they were trying to stop me from rebuilding my empire. I ended up renaming the A&M store after my big supermarket that was burnt down: Whitt's Discount Supermarket. I had a $3,500 grocery lift across the street which the city confiscated without my knowledge. Here's my next strategic move: I opened a new little store next to my club on Albany Avenue. I assumed that the FBI tapped my phone line at my house to see if I had anything to do with my store being burnt down. My lawyer and I had a four-day deposition with the insurance company.

Camelot Begins to Look a Little Bleak

Watching my father and family has caused me to have a deep sense of responsibility for those that have been assigned to me. I am a normal man who just believes there is more to life than what is "normal." I believe if you put your hand to the plow, you will come out ahead of the game. Our lives have been designed by the Creator of everything that is good. We have been told and assured that if we love God and our neighbors as ourselves, then we will have success.

For everything that I have achieved and lost as well, I am thankful beyond measure. As a man and a husband, at times I find it exceedingly difficult to view our current lives and see what I thought I would see. You see, life changes in the blink of eye right in front of our faces while we're looking in another direction. With our eyes wide open, we don't see what just happened. Is it because our eyes don't or will not see what they don't want to see?

The Empire
Starts to Fall

Standing upright and having done all to stand, I found that everything I had worked for was suddenly closing in on me, and I didn't understand what and why these things were happening. My life, my wife's life, my children's life, my employees' life became unglued. I had held the reins as the head, the leader, the one who would ensure that they, we, even me all would be quite well and fine. What was happening now was of monumental scope, and there was nothing I could do about it.

You're wondering what happened. I wondered too, my friend. My project for the supermarket that got so much press was a multi-million-dollar endeavor. I am who I am. I am a hardworking man. We hadn't yet adopted the "work smarter, not harder" mantra/concept. As a black man, what else was I to do but work hard for myself and family? I learned early on that if you wanted to get ahead, you had to go on ahead and get what you desired. We did this with no thoughts of limiting another or cheating someone out of their fair share. There were no dirty back-door dealings. Everything was decent and in order.

My store burnt down, or they burnt it down. Whichever it was, it started an avalanche of unexpected and debilitating occurrences. I was always accountable for managing what had been given to me. Our loans began to be in default, properties were beginning to be foreclosed, and suddenly the IRS was after us! We worked too hard to get to this point and have it all fall apart.

I had closed two of my three stores down when I opened my big discount store. After the fire, I reopened Roy's Grocery Store on Nelson Street and A&M Market on Albany Avenue so that we would have some income coming in. Luckily, the big discount store was only in business for about a month and a half, and I hadn't sold these two stores. I had to remodel and fix the stores up to get them ready to open for business.

Filing Chapter 11 bankruptcy was a slap in my face followed by ice-cold water being poured all over me. Everything went awry—I mean everything—for what seemed to be no reason whatsoever. I had bought my wife a beautiful car, a Cadillac, which she adored. The IRS attempted to seize my property from the store. They went so far as to put my truck on a lift truck in front of my nightclub, Unique Lounge. Luckily, I was inside the club when these things were happening. I quickly went outside to speak with the IRS officer to let him know I had filed Chapter 11. The officer went to confirm my information, and when he had confirmed what I said I had done, his tone changed. A bit of calm was restored, and my truck was unhooked from the tow truck.

We still had a degree of cash flow, but things were definitely different, quite different. I can't adequately explain the toll that these happenings had on us as a family, and especially what was happening between Anne and me. Court proceedings, depositions, and testimonies—what happened? Was I watching a movie?

More would happen. For instance, my attorney, Arnold Bayer, had an accident and was killed. Then my main advisor and trusted friend also passed away. It was truly too much to handle. These were fiery darts, and they were aimed dead at us. Finally, Anne and I separated. I moved away from our home, the lakefront property, on Lakeview Drive to an apartment over my store on Nelson Street.

On Sundays, the children—Nicole, Angela, and Roy Jr.—came to visit and spend some time with me. Thankfully, it wasn't long before Anne and I resumed our lives together as husband and wife. I was relieved. I returned home to West Hartford.

Anne is always there moving my life forward. We were separated for two months, which seemed like a lifetime.

And You Thought That Was Bad, Now See

We all have our strengths and weaknesses. Oftentimes we don't know why, where, or how they are developed. Rest is an essential need of the body, mind, and spirit.

I don't know what happened or why it happened; it just simply happened. No warning, no sign, no flashing lights, no reason. Just like breathing—inhale, exhale, it's involuntary.

I cannot tell you everything that happened because I don't know. What I can tell you is this: your life can change before you spell the *ch* in *change*. That's what happened to me. What I am about to share with you happened in such a powerful way. I must be likened to Job in this modern day. On that day, a day that would be as one like none before but the same as every day, I went as usual to close one of the stores.

Shall I say calamity or mayhem stepped up and introduced itself? Or was it the hand of the devourer? Was it God Almighty?

What it was I don't know, and I may never know.

One Saturday, I was outside doing some strenuous yard work. After working in the yard, I later left to close some of my stores. That next day, I got really sick. I thought to myself that I needed to lie down. I was tired, and I didn't feel well. I had never felt this way in my life. This feeling was very unfamiliar to me. I never felt this way before. It wasn't a feeling of general sickness at all. It was much more than that. But what I didn't know—here it was in July, and I was on the sofa covered up with a blanket. What was happening to me? My wife and the kids weren't home yet. I thought to myself, *Hopefully, they will get here soon. Something just wasn't right and I just wanted my family home with me.* Did I tell you that I love my family? I love them. Oh yes, I do. And they love me too.

Quite frankly, it became difficult for me to remember the rest of everything that would happen later. After some time, I do recall that Anne and the kids came home, and she began to prepare dinner. She asked me if I was ready to eat and wanted my dinner. I said, "Not right now."

Anne dozed off to sleep. Upon her waking up, she found me lying on the floor in the hallway of our home. *Lord, have mercy on me. Please have mercy on me.*

Anne immediately called 911 for help. The ambulance arrived and took me to the hospital, where I would stay in a coma for the next two months.

Life as We Know It Departs as the Sun Sets

My mother, Beatrice Whitt, and my sisters Deloris, Unzia, Essie, and Shirley came to visit me while I was in the hospital. They stayed at my brother's house. They didn't know what had happened to me and were very suspicious. This caused them not to be supportive of my wife or kids. They only visited me a couple of times in the entire journey that would become our new way of life. I was in intensive care, where rules of visitation were strict.

My so-called friends did not even visit me. The only one I ever remember visiting me was my friend Leo Collins. The doctors said it was impossible for me to live at that point. They said that if I did survive, I would be in a vegetative state for the rest of my life because my brain was considered dead for too long to make a full recovery. It was divine intervention that took place at that time because according to my wife, so many people were praying for me. One lady moved into our home with my wife and children and prayed day and night for my recovery. Her name was Mother Betrina Lawson.

After the amputations, Newington Children's Hospital was called, and David Jedwenski came to fit me for a prosthesis before I was sent to a New Britain Memorial for rehab. Then after having stayed at St. Francis for two months, I had to endure six months of rehabilitation. During the process of rehabilitation, I had to learn how to walk all over again, use my prosthesis, and how to use special gadgets that would enable me to use the bathroom.

Five days a week for six months, they woke me up at 7:00 a.m. to wash me. Around 8:00 a.m., they wheeled me to the dining room to have breakfast. Afterward, they wheeled me back to my room. Around 8:30 a.m., the nurses wheeled me down to have physical therapy. My wife had a phone installed in my room so that we could constantly keep in touch.

After church every Sunday, I looked forward to visits from my wife and children. At that time, she was busy overseeing two grocery stores, a nightclub, and a forty-two-unit apartment building, but still she took the time to visit me every day. I wondered to myself how she could do everything that she did. However, she assured me that it was Almighty God that helped her stay strong. And, also the help of Mother Lawson, with her continuous prayers and help with the children. My wife told me Mother Lawson was sent by God after I got sick to help her get though the situation. I didn't know Mother Lawson before I fell. On the weekends, my sister-in-law, Penny Harts, would come over and make breakfast while my wife, Anne, picked me up from the hospital on the weekends to spend time with our family. This took place for four months before I was able to come home indefinitely. I was transferred from New Britain Memorial back to Newington Children's Hospital for the final fitting of my prosthesis. There I had to learn how to open and close my myoelectric hands with my muscles.

Before I was transferred to Newington Hospital for my final fitting, my wife and I sat down with the *Hartford Courant* newspaper for an interview. To my stupidity, I refused an interview with my insurance company, which resulted in an increase in my insurance from $300 to $980 a month.

My excuse for declining the interview was that I was tired from the previous interview with the *Hartford Courant* newspaper. My insurance company had already paid almost a million dollars in hospital bills, which was their excuse for raising my insurance premium.

I was finally discharged after four months of staying at Newington Children's Hospital. Finally I was able to return home to West Hartford for good. Before I came home, my stepson LaRenzo and his son had moved into our house from South Carolina. LaRenzo was old enough to help his mother manage Roy's Grocery on Nelson Street.

About six months after I came home from the hospital, my stepson began taking me to work Monday through Friday for roughly seven years. The old saying "when the cat's away, the mice will play" literally stood true. My wife did her best to watch over things but unfortunately her eyes could not be everywhere. She had to juggle caring for me, her newly disabled husband, the kids, homelife and multiple businesses. Her eyes could not be everywhere and a lot of people including employees took advantage and ultimately caused the business to fail. They were breaking into the store so bad that my wife got her pistol and slept overnight inside the store. One night while she was sleeping in the store, someone tried to break in. She fired one shot, but did not hit the intruder.

Also, during the time that I was sick, my two daughters got out of control. They decided to steal my Mercedes Benz and went joy-riding with their friends. Someone spotted them driving on Bedford Street and called their mother. She then woke up out of her sleep to go looking for them and eventually found them. Afterward, my daughters went over to their aunt's house. One of my daughters stayed there for a week, and the other one stayed for a whole year. She ended up missing school for a year, but did finish. My wife's brother came from South Carolina. While he was here, he and another one of my wife's brothers had a talk with my daughters to get them to come back home.

My daughter that had missed school for a year had graduated with my younger daughter. Once she came home, she started working at the store on Nelson Street. In the meantime, bills were looming from the bankruptcy, so my wife took out a $175,000 loan against our personal home in West Hartford to help pay off some of the bills. They tried to foreclose on the eighteen-unit building on Albany Avenue. We paid the balance of $33,000 to save the building from foreclosure. A man by the name of George Swann came to the building and told the residents to pay him the rent and not pay my wife before the foreclosure took place. After all this chaos, we decided to leave Connecticut and bought a house in Hopkins. We borrowed $100,000 from the eighteen-unit building on Albany Avenue to put down on the $300,000 home in Hopkins. The owner of the house gave us two years to pay off the balance of $200,000 under the condition that we sell the building on Albany Avenue.

Once we purchased the house in Hopkins, South Carolina, my wife's sister and family moved into the house while we were still in Connecticut. My wife sent one of my daughters down to Hopkins to stay in the house with her aunt while my other daughter stayed in Connecticut. Soon after, my son went down to Hopkins to stay with his sister. They stayed there for two years and came back to Connecticut. We ended up losing the house in Hopkins because we didn't meet the deadline for paying off the $200,000. We didn't sell the building on Albany Avenue in time to pay off the $200,000. The $175,000 loan mentioned earlier, which was going to be used to pay off the bills for bankruptcy, still needed to be paid. We closed the store on Nelson Street, and we did not have any income coming in to pay toward the $175,000 loan. This forced the finance company to foreclose on our home in West Hartford. After this happened, we moved out of that house and moved in with my wife's sister in Bloomfield, Connecticut, for about six months.

One of the other reasons for me buying the Unique Lounge club was because I had already bought all my grocery stores and apartment buildings, and it was time for me to enjoy some of my hard work. I had about thirty employees, and they could come together and mingle with one another after a hard day's work. My employees enjoyed the discount of purchasing anything for $1. Unfortunately, things changed when I got sick and had to go to the hospital. My wife was not a club person but rather a churchgoing woman. She ultimately had to depend on the employees to run the business. They took advantage of the situation and stole as they saw fit. Eventually, this put us out of business.

This caused my wife to lease the business for $25,000 to a gentleman on the assumption that when he got the business up and running, he would buy the building. He kept the business open for about two years, but he could not make suitable profit, so he closed it. Then another person came along, and my wife ended up renting the business, hoping he could get it up and going and be able to buy the building. He opened it up for a while but, unfortunately again, could not make a profit. We had to evict him from the premises.

In the meantime, he had spent some money on the property, forging my wife's name on some of the paperwork, stating that she gave him the okay to do the work on the building. We eventually had to go to court to fulfill the eviction. And of course, at the last minute, he did not show up in court, and the judge granted the eviction. He had no choice but to move out. He brazenly forged my wife's name again on some paperwork saying that she had sold him the building. That gave him the opportunity to file for moving the liquor license from our location to another location without our knowledge. We were blindsided, but luckily, we found out in time, which allowed us to save our license for the building. Fortunately, another gentleman approached my wife, and we ended up selling him the business and building for $80,000.

After all this mishap, we decided to try moving to South Carolina again, where my wife's sister ended up leasing a home in Columbia, South Carolina. My credit was so bad that we had to assume the mortgage. The house cost $120,000, and we put down $25,000. We rented two moving trucks to move our things to South Carolina.

My wife, myself, and our grandson flew on the airplane while my sons and nephew drove the moving trucks. We eventually sold the building on Albany Avenue for $500,000 and took back a second mortgage for $180,000. When the mortgage ballooned on the building on Albany Avenue, the new owner stopped making payments to us. Somehow or another, he buddied up with our former lawyer at that time, which caused us to have to hire another lawyer to get our money.

When we moved to South Carolina, I was glad to leave Connecticut and all the bad luck. I wanted a brand-new start away from all the chaos. After we were settled into our new home, it was great for a time. Before too long had passed, I began to start missing my old surroundings. Being that I was in a new place and handicapped, it was hard to make new friends because I left my old friends behind. Also, being handicapped was a challenge in making new friends because I could not get out and about to spend time with others when I wanted to. There were people that I thought wanted to be my friend. However, I found out that they had other intentions. What kept me going was putting my faith into the Lord and seeking His grace.

From 1984 to 2010 when I decided to write this book, having relocated to the South with my wife, one son, and grandson and realizing that I left my three daughters in Connecticut, things had turned too many times for me to feel any degree of comfort or satisfaction with myself as a provider for my family. It was difficult for me to accept having gone from owning over a million-dollar corporation to seemingly now being in an unfamiliar situation and location that I was not accustomed to. The demands of this on me as a man who prided himself in being an excellent provider to his family caused me to look at everything in a different light.

And what seemed to be adding insult to injury was the fact that I lost my limbs and now depended on my wife, son, and grandson to do for me what I couldn't do for myself.

In 1993, my wife went to work for her brother, who owned a refrigeration business, Anne worked as his secretary. She didn't know how to operate a computer, so she took it upon herself to learn on her own. With the assistance of a soon-to-be retired secretary, she bought her first computer. Before long, it came to a point where the kids were grown and moved out, and I had to learn how to do these things for myself. I got tired of asking my wife to comb my hair, so what did I do? I designed a special tool that my son made for me which would allow me to comb my own hair. I can now use the microwave oven to fix my own meals, and I can even wash certain parts of my body as well as change my own clothes. I can also use the restroom by myself and stay by myself for a period. I exercise by walking about two hours a day and doing three thousand stomach push-ups. I can put on my upper prosthetics, but my wife has to put my lower ones on for me. I can get in the bed by myself.

One thing I've truly come to understand and fully appreciate is how essential those little things are that we often take for granted without ever realizing their value. It takes little hinges to keep up a whole structure. My little hinges were taken away, and now I see better.

God is holding me together, and I do believe in some small way that I am at my best self now. I wouldn't have always said that. God has not forsaken me. By His grace and mercy, I am still viable. Albeit at times, I wonder about my being the best husband to my wife. Anne is more than an exceptional woman. She is better than phenomenal; she is a gift that only Jesus could have known I would need. It pains me still to this day that she has had to endure this more than I have. A woman always knows, and Anne knows more than I ever will. How can I be to her what I've always wanted to be for her? I still seek God, asking for a way to reach out to her to touch her like she has touched my life and heart. I am not certain I deserve her. It's has not even been fair for her. Her life was lost just as much as my life was lost when they removed my limbs. She's beautiful and kind. She's an inspiration that I hope will be inspired to continue believing in what God does for us and through us, all for His glory. I think Anne knows God's heart; that's why she's still here, just as strong and stable as always more than forty-five years later of having said "I do." And she has gone above and beyond for the "in sickness and in health" always in all ways.

If you have a spouse or a significant other and you're about to embark upon marriage, let me encourage you to provide your heart to your intended, for there may come a day when that's all you have to give to them. Ask me, I am a man who has learned this in the most unusual manner. Hug and love frequently, for they mean much as you listen to their heartbeat.

I was able to survive for thirty-eight years without losing my mind by putting my trust into the Lord every day, praying and reading my Bible. The television kept me entertained as well. About ten years after I moved to South Carolina, my memory began coming back to me in stages. I started feeling not so well, so I made an appointment with my doctor. He took blood tests and referred me to a specialist, where they took a biopsy. The biopsy revealed that I had prostate cancer. The doctor who diagnosed me with prostate cancer referred me to another doctor. He immediately wanted to operate when he received the information. My wife and I were unsure about having the operation, so we went to another doctor and got a second opinion. After talking with the second doctor, we decided to go with the radiation treatments. I had to go through approximately two and a half months of radiation treatment at the hospital, spending one hour per treatment session once per week.

My mother passed away on September 2, 2002. We buried her next to the church where my father was buried in the Whitts' cemetery. She had forty acres of land and two acres of land where the house sat, which she willed to the kids. I got her seventy-year-old bedroom set. After about nineteen years, my mind started coming back to me. I started a new merchandise business through the internet!

My next-door neighbor, Reverend Wade, came over to meet me when he bought his house. He was a chaplain in the army and became a pastor of his own church. At the beginning, he would come over to our house and pray for us and serve communion once a month. He ended up taking on a second church and became very busy. After this happened, he sent his deacons over to serve us communion instead. My son, Roy Jr., got married in October of 2008 to my daughter-in-law Sabrina Coe and started his own family. Like a chip off the old block, he started his own business: a vending company.

In the meantime, my daughter Nicole set me up an e-mail account because she knew that I would eventually need it. This e-mail account was set up through her phone for her to monitor my incoming messages. This enabled me to start a business with my daughter's help online. If anything needed to be done for the online business, I called her for assistance. However, I knew that it was beginning to become overwhelming trying to handle my situation and her life as well. I turned to my wife for help at this point.

Unfortunately, my wife was also extremely busy with her own work. This led me to believe that I would not be able to operate my business due to their busy schedules. I began to think of ways on how I could possibly operate a computer with my prosthetics, not being able to fully control a mouse. As the years went by, if I needed to order anything online for the business I had to ask one of them.

Afterward, my daughter, Nicole, set up an eBay account for me so that I would be able to sell my products online. She wanted me to excel with my online business through eBay so that I could get back into business as I was before I lost my arms and legs. In the meantime, I decided to purchase my own computer without knowing how to operate it. I ended up calling my grandson LaRenzo to go and purchase me a laptop computer. Once I received my computer, he set it up for me, only to find out that I couldn't use the mouse on the laptop. So my wife purchased a large external mouse for ease of use. This still proved difficult to use as it jumped all over the place, but I was determined to figure it out.

It took too long for me to position the mouse in the location I needed it to be in, so my grandson purchased a device with voice-command features, but I was unable to get it to work right. One day I was watching TV when a commercial showed a woman operating a computer with her stumps. Shortly afterward, I removed my prosthesis and began using the laptop with my stumps. This was the best thing that could have ever happened to me.

After learning how to use my stumps to operate my laptop, my grandson set me up with a Facebook account. This allowed me to reconnect with a lot of my relatives and friends. Currently, I am ordering products online myself and have also set up a trading account online. Praise to the Lord that He is good all the time!

Anne's Report

Anne

Can I start with a very deep and long sigh? Can I recant what happened during those days in July, August, and September? Those were the two months that Roy was in a coma. How long was it with no communication with my husband? It was too long to be long. What it was, was a life-altering experience that has forever changed the way we love, live, breathe, and even the way we pray and the way we don't pray just as much.

> *Likewise the Spirit also helps in our weaknesses.*
> *For we do not know what we should pray for as we*
> *ought, but the Spirit Himself makes intercession*
> *for us with groanings which cannot be uttered.*
> —Romans 8:26

Marriage vows are promises each partner in a couple makes to the other during a wedding—to have and to hold, from this day forward, for better, for worse, for richer, for poorer, *in sickness and in health*, until death do us part. And so on this beautiful Sunday, July 1, 1984, a hot day in July, the children and I came home from church to find my husband on the couch covered up in a blanket. From the

911 call until this day, it still seems unreal to me. Our lives as we knew it would never be the same.

A few days ago, my husband was standing tall, a strong, vibrant, healthy man. Never sick, not even with a cold. As my small children and I entered the hospital every day after school, I began to watch my husband deteriorate before my eyes. I begged God, *Please don't let my husband die. You gave him to me, and now You are going to take him from me? Not now.* We were so young and had so much living to do. So many places to go. We had big plans for our future. This couldn't be happening.

I watched my husband's flesh fall off his body. His body seemed to be rotting. The room smelled like a body that was decomposing. His temperature was so high, and his body broke out in boils, which caused his flesh to fall off as the boils burst open. I recalled the story of Job in the Bible, and I realized that this was so similar. Through all of this, I learned—I mean really learned—how to pray.

There was a powerful woman I had met a couple of years back, and she became my mother. I called her and told her what was happening, and she said, "I'll be there tomorrow." Her name was Betrina Lawson, known as Evangelist Lawson or Mother Lawson. Mother Lawson became a real mother to me. I felt so much better when she said she was coming. She prayed day and night for us. She fasted for weeks. I felt closer to God when I was around her because she exuded so much of the love of God. It was catching, and I knew she loved me like a daughter. I soon learned about the love from your family and friends. Most of them turned. Then lies started flowing. People were using Bibles, saying they were preachers just to get into the room to see my husband and spread rumors because they didn't understand. They didn't understand why his hands and legs were amputated. The blood had stopped flowing to those parts of his body, and gangrene set in, so the amputations had to take place. Did they ask? *No.*

Long story short, what I needed was my family and friends. All but a few vanished. I have been my husband's caregiver for thirty-five years now. Only with the help of God that I have found new friends—reasons to continue this journey. It's not at all easy. But thanks be to God for the great people that God has placed in my life. It's lighter for me. I just must praise my God for making a way for me and my children because there were times when I would cry for days, thinking, *I can't do this anymore.* But I would remember my vows for better or worse. Richer or poorer. In sickness and in health. Until death do us part. So I am holding up my end of the bargain. I'll stop here because my book will be forthcoming.

The hurt doesn't hurt anymore because God has given me a forgiving heart—to forgive all the lies that were told, how I was treated and still am treated by those who said they loved me and were there when we were rich, but when we became poor, they fled like we had the plague.

So no matter the outcome in your life, no matter the downfalls, the setbacks, the troubles, remember this: *never, never give up.*

Roy and I experienced and continue to experience all-the-above marriage vows for God's glory. We are forever united as one. We are singleness of purpose in this earthly realm. We remain true to what God has called us to do and be, albeit at times, I believe I had thoughts of not hearing and heeding to do what I know I was created to do, and that is to love and comfort without regard to my own needs. I don't imagine it would be correct to not admit that I did struggle with the challenges and the anger and loneliness that left me feeling helpless and frightened too. I had the children to care for; I had Roy to care for.

> *Therefore a man shall leave his father*
> *and mother and be joined to his wife,*
> *and they shall become one flesh.*
> —Genesis 2:24

I was so distraught that I honestly didn't know what or why these things happened and how long they would stay this way. No answers came from the doctors about Roy's condition. They still didn't know what was wrong with him.

Roy didn't know Roy, I don't think. He had escaped the hustle and the bustle. He was always working so hard. He loved the work that he did and the legacy that he was trying to build. Oftentimes,

I thought that he worked too hard but he was driven to accomplish everything that he set his mind to accomplish. That is one of the things that I admire about him.

The schedule to keep watch over Roy was daunting and draining to me. I kept the faith and the face of contentment with what was going on, believing that God was in control—and that this would all be over soon.

People sure had been supportive, and some were suspect, and some secretly looked as if they enjoyed hearing reports of Roy's condition. There was no improvement at all. Why did they have that smirk on their faces with a side-eye glance? I received many questions: *How was everything going? When was Roy coming home?*

The Diagnosis Arrives

After many extensive and grueling tests, false starts and beyond, the doctors provided the diagnosis of Roy's condition: *meningococcal meningitis.*

What? What in the world is that, Doctor?

Meningitis is an inflammation of the protective layer around the brain and spinal cord. This inflammation can be caused by a virus, a bacterium, or even a fungus.

> ➤ *Viral meningitis* is the most common form. It is serious but generally not life threatening, and it usually goes away in seven to ten days.

> ➤ *Bacterial meningitis* is rare, but it is very serious and potentially fatal. It includes meningococcal disease.

Meningococcal meningitis is caused by the bacterium called meningococcus. In addition to meningitis, meningococcus can cause other serious infections. For example, it can enter the bloodstream and cause an infection called meningococcal sepsis. Meningococcal disease, which includes both meningococcal meningitis and meningococcal sepsis, can progress quickly. It can make an infant or teenager very sick and may even be life threatening.

A New Way of Living Begins

Anne

In the words of the late Reverend Dr. Martin Luther King Jr.,

> The ultimate measure of a man is not where he stands in moments of comfort and convenience, but where he stands at times of challenge and controversy.

> Faith is taking the first step even when you don't see the whole staircase.

These words epitomize my husband, Roy's, journey of a thousand miles. Roy has a will that is made of bendable steel. Roy Whitt is a man that knows that he can do all things through Christ who strengthens him.

For every individual who took time to come look see, they will see that Roy went through a portal that not many men would be able to come out of on the right side with his heart still intact. Sure, there are days when they are too long and nights when they are too short. However, through every day, Roy lifts his eyes to his Lord and Savior, Jesus the Christ.

Roy was always a tall man, standing about six feet four. He was physically quick and agile. Nowadays, Roy is still standing six feet four but in a different manner. Roy stands with God, and it is the Lord that keeps him lifted, standing strong and tall beyond the eyes that watch and wonder.

Roy has found that the Lord is his shield and buckler. As for me, I am still in awe of the measure of man that Roy is. There were days when I wanted to disappear, to just evaporate. Then I remembered, where would Roy be?

After forty-seven years of marriage, we are still surrounded by love and joy. Sure, challenges exist, but Roy is determined to *never give up*, and neither will I.

For you see, love is more than money, stuff, and contraptions to bind and hinder. Love is a man and his wife.

Here we are, Lord. Here we are. Use us for Your glory.

Love is what God has prepared for everyone who calls upon Him not only in times of trials and tribulation but also in times when the grandbabies laugh and old friends become reacquainted with one another—when good times are bad and when bad times are good—love never fails to be love.

Standing Tall

Here I am, Roy L. Whitt Sr. standing tall yet again, this time with the total help of the Lord. I've stepped out of the way and let Him have His way in me.

My wife, Anne, the lovely and ever special love of my life, stands with and by me day in and day out. Thank You, Lord, for this beautiful and incomparable partner who has renewed my joy in living daily for You. Please grant her the desires of heart, for surely she must be weary of these matters. Yet she never seems to show it at all. What a lucky and blessed man I am.

My wife was going through some old letters that she had come across. One of the letters was from my daughter Nicole and Angela's pastor, Pastor Alicia Greer. In the letter, she was prophesizing to my wife that I would be using a computer. This prophecy came to be in 2012!

Never Give Up!

He who finds a wife finds a good thing,
And obtains favor from the LORD.
—Proverbs 18:22

Though I no longer have my extremities, I've come to realize and accept the fact that life is in the center of what matters most—my heart, and it is full and rich with not a single degree of malice or thoughts of being less than I am, which is God's son.

Roy Whitt

*"For I know the plans I have for you," declares
the LORD, "plans to prosper you and not to harm
you, plans to give you hope and a future."*
—Jeremiah 29:11 NIV

I never knew it would be so, but God sure did!

If He did it for us, He'll do it for you too!
You can count on Him!

May our Lord and Savior Jesus the Christ bless you abundantly!

Never, never, never give up!

About the Author

Roy Whitt is the man who many didn't think would make it out of his hospital bed alive some thirty-eight years ago. Armed with $20, a bus pass, and big dreams, he migrated from the Deep South to New England in search of a better life for himself. Who would have known that a farmer's son with only a high school diploma would be able to create an incredibly successful business in such a short period of time? His story is riveted with both triumph and tragedy, but most importantly—one of the most potent doses of never giving up!

CPSIA information can be obtained
at www.ICGtesting.com
Printed in the USA
LVHW052205270121
677519LV00008B/263